PROTEUS
London & New York

VISIONS OF ROCK

'I'...e before I'm very old...
don't know why, I just h...
this feeling. There have b...
plenty of other times ...
nearly died.'

needle go in. We had n...
fixation.
Although both Nancy ar...
kicked the heroin ...
hear the ...
hand ...
he...

Sid
Vicious
died of
a heroin
overdose
tasteless
pathetic

"We're anti-fascist,
anti-violence, anti-racist. We're
against ignorance."
(Joe Strummer, The Clash)

Blondie

What is BILLY IDOL'S
dark secret?

SHA...

all
THE

SEX

COMPILED BY
MAL BURNS

Visions of Rock

Produced by Media & Graphic Creations (Graphixus Editions)
for Proteus Books. **PROTEUS BOOKS** is an imprint of the
Proteus Publishing Group.

United States:	**PROTEUS PUBLISHING CO., INC.** 733, Third Avenue New York, NY – 10017
Distributed by:	**THE SCRIBNER BOOK COMPANIES, INC.** 597, Fifth Avenue New York, NY – 10017
United Kingdom:	**PROTEUS (PUBLISHING) LIMITED,** Bremar House Sale Place London, W2 1PT

ISBN: 0 906071 42 9 (softbound)

First published in the United Kingdom in March 1981.
First published in the United States in June 1981.
© Copyright 1981 Media & Graphic Creations.
All rights reserved.

For foreign and co-edition rights please contact Proteus Books.

For merchandising and other rights please contact
Media & Graphic Creations,
38 Mount Pleasant
London, WC1 X 0AP, United Kingdom.
Telex: 261177 – PANSEC.G.

Book compiled by Mal Burns.
Book designed by David Noon.

All individual contents are copyright 1981
the credited writers and illustrators.

Printed and bound by Jolly & Barber Ltd., Rugby, England.

"VISIONS OF ROCK" LOGOTYPE DESIGN BY ANGUS McKIE.

COVER ILLUSTRATION BY ALAN CRADDOCK

INTRODUCTION

    If Olivia Newton John and Johnny Rotten met on a bus, I doubt they'd have much to say to each other. It's hard to imagine two more disparate performers, yet VISIONS OF ROCK is equally concerned with both.

    It is a book about images, the abstract quality of public appeal that influences us to follow one artist and not another. Everyone is aware of it, whether it has been carefully manufactured by an astute manager and record company or is seemingly spontaneous – a natural expression of someone's personality. Olivia Newton John might seem to be the untouchable dream-girl, frothy and synthetic, whereas to many, Johnny Rotten, consistently outrageous and belligerently independent, is the perfect anti-star. Either way it is their image that is important. It's hard to analyse; obviously it's largely based on a style of music but it is also clothes, posturing and attitudes. Illustration is the perfect medium to capture the essence of each performer's image as it can interpret and explore, providing an insight into the rock persona in a way that photography never could.

VISIONS OF ROCK is an illustrated statement on current trends in music from Disco to New Wave based on the particular fascination of a number of top artists from the fields of comic books, commercial graphics and the music press.

Because of the vast scope of the subject matter, it is inevitable that some favorites will have been omitted in an attempt to provide as coherent as possible a cross-section of present-day talent.

The artists themselves have been given free rein to develop their own slants on particular acts that inspire them, and so the resulting pictures vary not only in style but in their critical thrust and use of symbolism, providing a range from savage satire to glowing accolade. This disparity has meant that in some cases more than one view of a certain performer has been included, knowing that members of an audience relate in a number of different ways to any one artist.

This apparently random quality is also the book's strength. The range of creative vision shown makes it an art book, and rock followers will be intrigued to see how those, who may not be their chosen idols, have been treated.

The visual material has been complemented by the concise, sometimes slightly acerbic, captions of Tim Lott, whose opinions are necessarily tempered by having for many years watched the fluctuations of the rock business from the inside. Ex-editor of *Record Mirror* in England, free-lance journalist and present editor of *Flexipop,* he has attempted to provide a slick summary of the appeal of each subject.

VISIONS OF ROCK has been divided into five sections: the first two spotlight foremost solo artists and bands respectively; the third is devoted to the monolithic memory of those often referred to as 'rock legends'; the fourth clears the stage for a group that might be termed 'cult' performers and the last resorts to wild comic exaggeration.

VISIONS OF ROCK aims to make a comment; it will provoke some and delight others.

On second thoughts I can't picture Olivia Newton John on a bus in the first place.

NICOLAS LOCKE

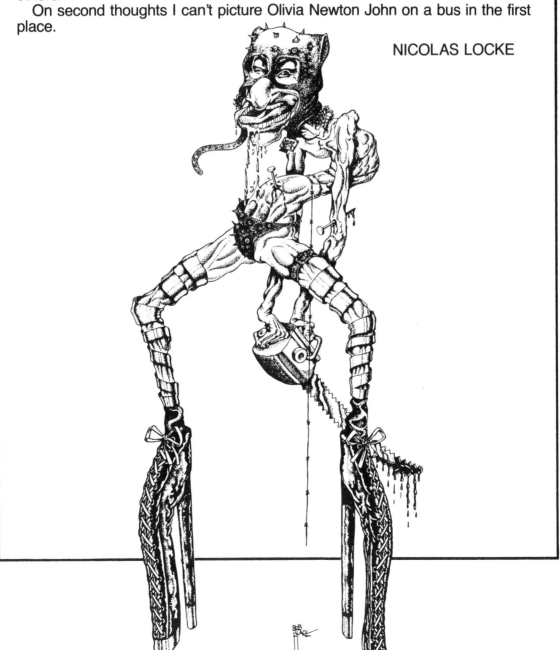

THE SUPER STARS

ILLUSTRATION BY BORIN VAN LOON

DAVID BOWIE

ILLUSTRATION BY CHRIS PRIESTLEY

Bowie . . . hollow cheeked chameleon with crippled eye and the soaring vision . . . stylish, synthetic sybarite of the AC/DC set . . . copied by many . . . adored by all.

ILLUSTRATION BY IAN SANDER

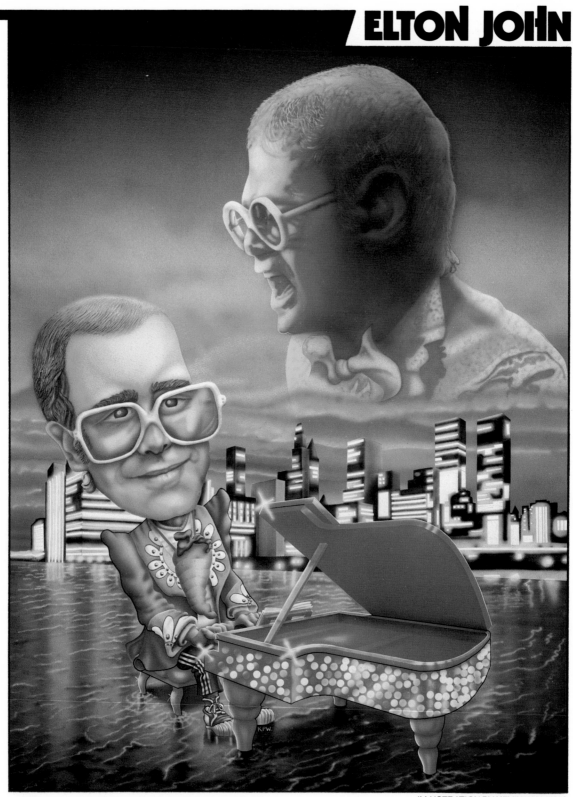

ILLUSTRATION BY KEVIN WILLIAMS

Elton . . . four eyes, too outrageous and one for the road . . . ageing but evergreen . . . balding but beautiful . . . chubby but charismatic . . . the six million dollar man, at least.

ILLUSTRATION BY ALIGHERIO GUISSEPPETTI

GARY NUMAN

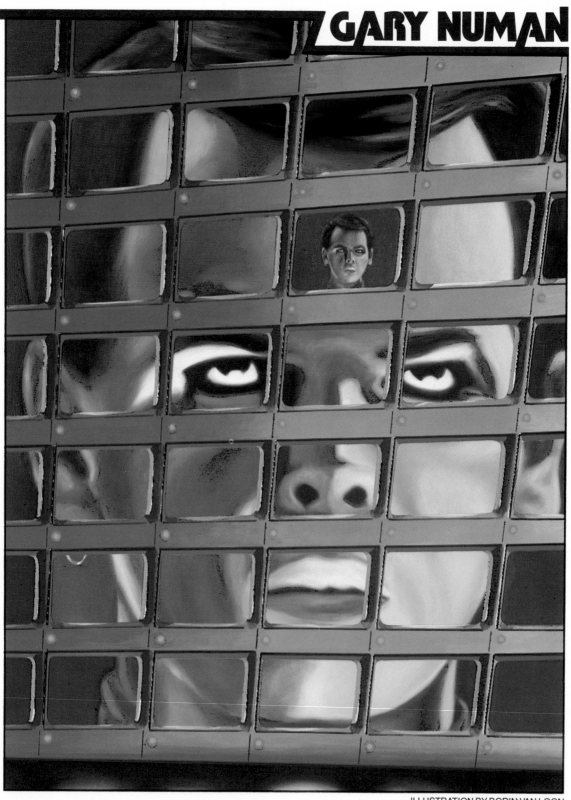

Numan . . . portly white duke of mascara music . . . space suits and the sound of computers . . . the young man's Bowie.

BRYAN FERRY

ILLUSTRATION BY BRETT EWINS

Ferry . . . languid lounge lizard with the quivering quiff and lachrymose larynx . . . paid by a million sophisticats in silk stockings and women too.

IAN DURY

ILLUSTRATION BY GUY LAWLEY
WITH COLOR BY BRETT EWINS

Dury . . . the rock 'n' roll brickie . . . the flat cap and grizzled jaw . . . voice of sawdust and phlegm . . . every inch the guvnor . . . every inch an oik.

ELVIS COSTELLO

ILLUSTRATION BY STUART BRIERS

*Costello . . . the man with the golden sneer . . .
specs appeal and borrowed Buddy Holly bruises . . .
twisted genius and a victim of hate . . . the voice of
the rejected.*

PHIL LYNOTT & BOB GELDOF

ILLUSTRATION BY ALAN CRADDOCK

Lynott . . . the black Irishman with charm, poise
and poison in his voice . . . bass strut and Hendrix
high hair . . . the urchin with the gold teeth. Geldof . . .
he of big lips, big mouth and big ego . . . rock 'n' roll's
own Oscar Wilde . . . punk turned popstar . . .
popstar turned pretty boy.

ROD STEWART

ILLUSTRATION BY ALIGHERIO GUISSEPPETTI

Rod . . . roughshod vocals riding over saccharin melody and searing rock . . . the voice against the grain . . . the ugliest pretty boy in the world.

RITCHIE BLACKMORE

ILLUSTRATION BY ALAN CRADDOCK

Blackmore . . . antediluvian axeman with a penchant for ribald riffs and deafening decibels . . . created a rainbow from a throbbing purple . . . a taste in suspenders and black stockings.

BRUCE SPRINGSTEEN

ILLUSTRATION BY COLIN WILSON

Springsteen . . . the switchblade metro hero with the five o'clock shadow voice . . . a latter-day James Dean . . . a teenage dream but ageing rapidly.

ILLUSTRATION BY MARK MANNING

Rotten . . . an Oliver laced with vinegar . . . the man who put the pist in Pistols . . . red haired rheumy Rufus who influenced an entire generation with arnarchistic anecdotes . . . the survivor. Vicious . . . the memory.

BOB DYLAN

ILLUSTRATION BY STUART BRIERS

Dylan . . . the warbler who saw the light and lost his way . . . the paunchy poet who made the sixties shine with cute couplets and dimestore rhymes.

ILLUSTRATION BY PAUL SOWDAN

Kate . . . big lips, big hips and big tips . . . a remarkable pair of tonsils that jump up and down every time she walks . . . the English rose without a thorn in sight.

ILLUSTRATION BY DAVID NOON

ILLUSTRATION BY KEVIN WILLIAMS

Olivia . . . 1000 watt smile . . . cosmetic promise and apple-pie charm . . . look but don't touch.

DONNA SUMMER

ILLUSTRATION BY ALAN CRADDOCK

*Donna . . . kissco disco merchant with a neat line
in simulated vinyl orgasms . . . elevated to superstar
status and a chance to sing with Streisand.*

ILLUSTRATION BY STUART BRIERS

*Patti . . . batty, natty and tatty . . . the poet princess
of the parking lot . . . an integral part of the Big Apple
twilight zone.*

THE SUPER GROUPS

ILLUSTRATION BY BORIN VAN LOON

ILLUSTRATION BY BRETT EWINS

*Blondie . . . pure popsicles for now people . . .
punk for voyeurs with keyhole eyes . . . a kiddies'
Diana Dors in Debbie.*

ILLUSTRATION BY GUY LAWLEY
WITH COLOR BY BRETT EWINS

*Debbie Harry . . . the venus in blue jeans . . .
mellifluous Monroe of the new wave . . . the ultimate
in the pubescent schoolboy's fantasy.*

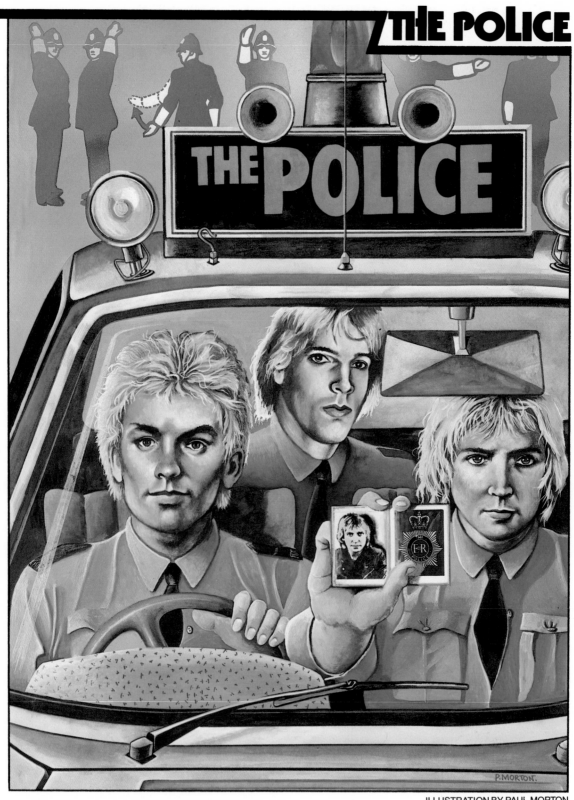

THE POLICE

ILLUSTRATION BY PAUL MORTON

*Police . . . the band that launched a thousand hits
. . . diluted reggae for the caucasian masses . . . the
Walker Brothers of the eighties.*

ILLUSTRATION BY JOHN HIGGINS

Sting . . . lead singer and guitarist . . . a male Debbie Harry . . . one policeman's ball that every girl would like to party . . . the pretty boy with the dirty voice.

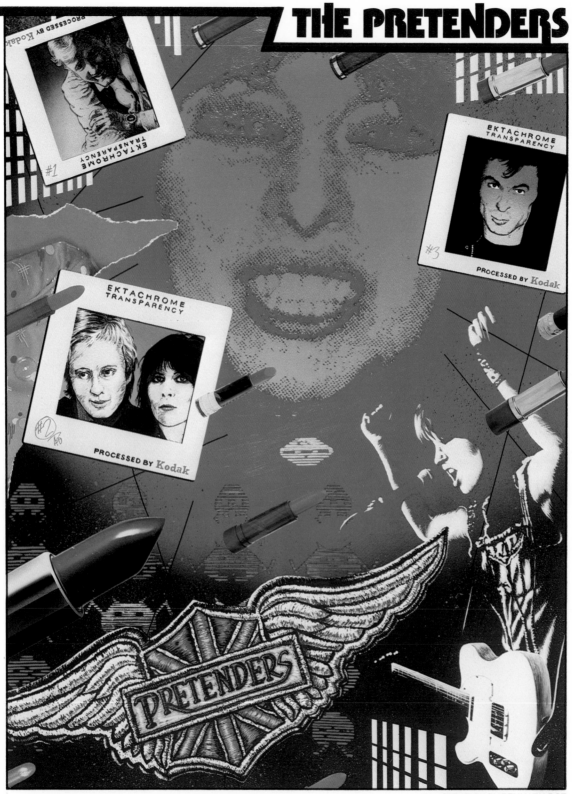

ILLUSTRATION BY BRYAN TALBOT

*Pretenders . . . the dirtier Blondie . . . neat tunes
for tomorrow's world fanatics . . . ice in the sun.*

ILLUSTRATION BY STUART BRIERS

Chrissie Hynde . . . the lead Pretender . . . a dollop of black ice cream for hair . . . a pair of lithe limbs for legs . . . erotic eyes, cute nose and the hollow cheeks . . . a forties film starlet from the backstreets.

ILLUSTRATION BY PAUL MORTON

*Yes . . . the acceptable face of the hippie rich . . .
no more, no less.*

THE CLASH

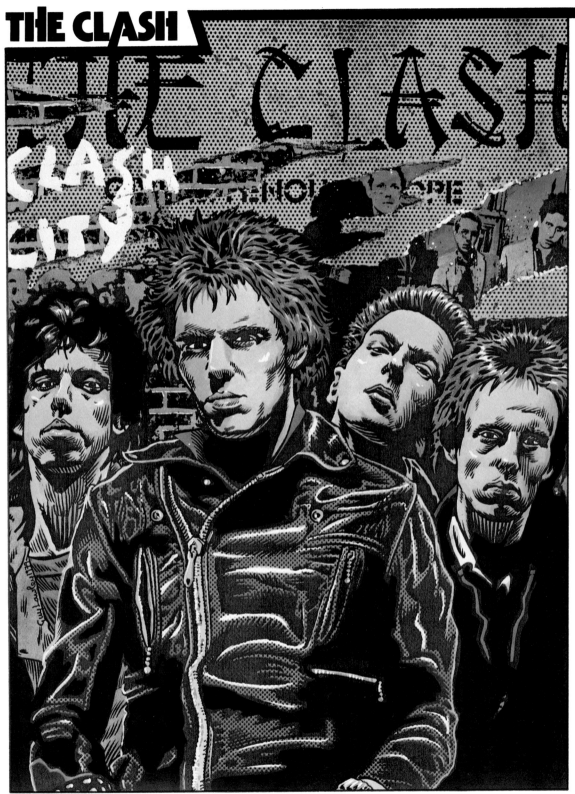

ILLUSTRATION BY GUY LAWLEY
WITH COLOR BY BRETT EWINS

The Clash . . . a bash with the flash . . . volatile and vicious . . . regular power station band with a cattle cult following .

ILLUSTRATION BY NEAL ADAMS

The Who . . . still crazy after all these years. The late Keith Moon . . . maniac drummer with the wall of sound for a heavy generation.

ROLLING STONES

ILLUSTRATION BY JOHN HIGGINS

(from the collection of Ms Mary Connolly)

*The Stones . . . rock 'n' roll's oldest hooligans . . .
never going to seed and always fulfilling a need . . .
hard music for the underbelly of pop.*

ILLUSTRATION BY IAN SANDER

Rush . . . Banshees encased in an electronic cocoon . . . the pipers at the gates of dawn . . . controlled hysteria and visions of fantasy.

ELO

ILLUSTRATION BY KEVIN O'NEILL

Electric Light Orchestra . . . bright sparks of the neo-classical . . . strings with wings . . . melody with molasses.

ILLUSTRATION BY ALAN CRADDOCK

Zeppelin . . . first and foremost of the heavy metal monsters . . . the Muhammed Ali's of rock.

KISS

ILLUSTRATION BY FLOYD HUGHES
AND DAVID HORNSBY

*Kiss . . . facepaint flamingos with tongues of fire
and licks of raw power . . . the biggest of spectacles
. . . the wildest of dreams.*

THE STRANGLERS

ILLUSTRATION BY DAVID MITCHELL

Stranglers . . . rock 'n' roll vermin with shadow beards . . . booming bass lines and keyboard crescendos . . . the four musketeers of macho rock . . . dark men dressed in black.

THE ROCK LEGENDS

ILLUSTRATION BY JOHN HIGGINS

ILLUSTRATION BY CLIFF HARPER

Jim Morrison . . . the lizard king . . . lewd and booed . . . crude and sued . . . a true legend . . . a prophet of doom with a zoom lens.

JIMI HENDRIX

ILLUSTRATION BY ALAN CRADDOCK

Jimi . . . he oozed cascading chords and nihilistic notes . . . his breath-taking barnet blew people's minds . . . zonked out and honked up, he conked out.

SID VICIOUS

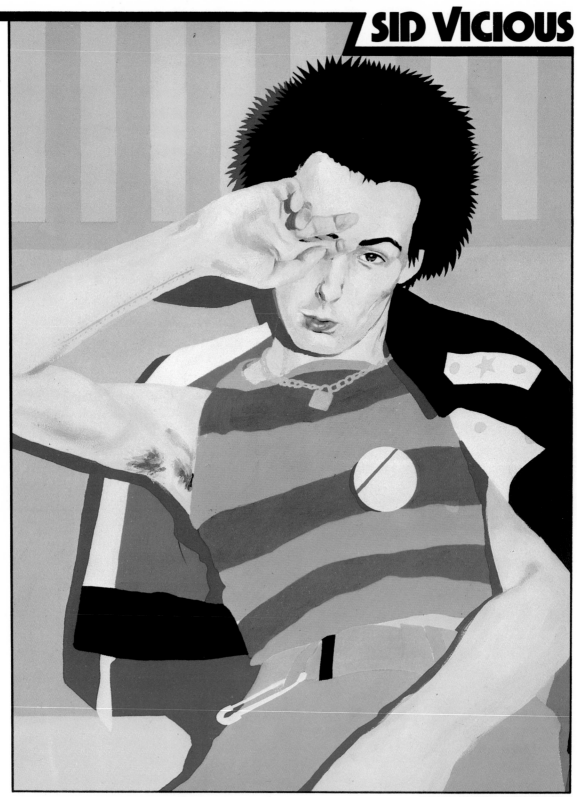

ILLUSTRATION BY CHRIS PRIESTLY

Vicious . . . spikey haired warrior who drowned in a sea of spit and smack . . . a human circus . . . the walking masochistic maisma who did it his way and lost . . . pumped himself full of five star dopes but only had a three star engine.

CULT FAVORITES

ILLUSTRATION BY CHRIS PRIESTLEY

ILLUSTRATION BY BORIN VAN LOON

*Third World . . . ebony soul warriors . . . ethnic
vengeance and the ultimate frontier for funk.*

THE SLITS

ILLUSTRATION BY BORIN VAN LOON

Slits . . . little boys in female bodies . . . mud-slinging provocation and simulated stimulation.

SIOUXSIE SIOUX

Siouxsie...nocturnal creature with the light owl eyes and a bitter grin...the despondent poetess and curvacious ice maiden, with the original Banshees.

ILLUSTRATION BY GUY LAWLEY
WITH COLOR BY BRETT EWINS

THE JAGS

ILLUSTRATION BY BRYAN TALBOT

Jags . . . Costello clones within the bins . . .
favorites of a newer new wave . . . future unknown.

TOYAH WILLCOX

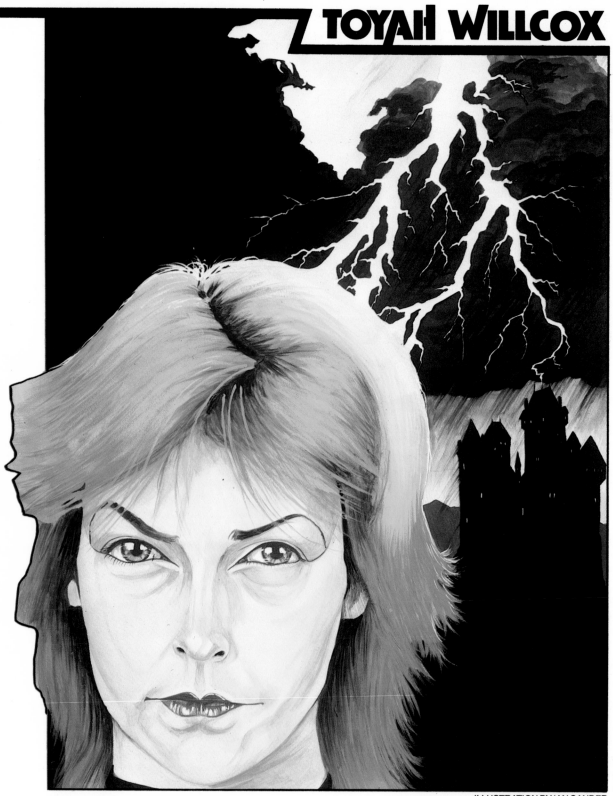

ILLUSTRATION BY IAN SANDER

Toyah Willcox . . . the elastic voice with a highly changeable hairstyle . . . new sophisto punk for the coffee table set.

HOWARD DEVOTO

Devoto . . . ex-Buzzcock now fronting a magazine . . . cold eerie sounds . . . echoes of a bleak future.

ILLUSTRATION BY NICK SPENDER

Sparks . . . flying into the electronic age with sheaths of synthesisers . . . square-jawed and gimlet eye . . . no town is big enough for both of them.

THE LIGHTER SIDE

ILLUSTRATION BY BOB HOARE

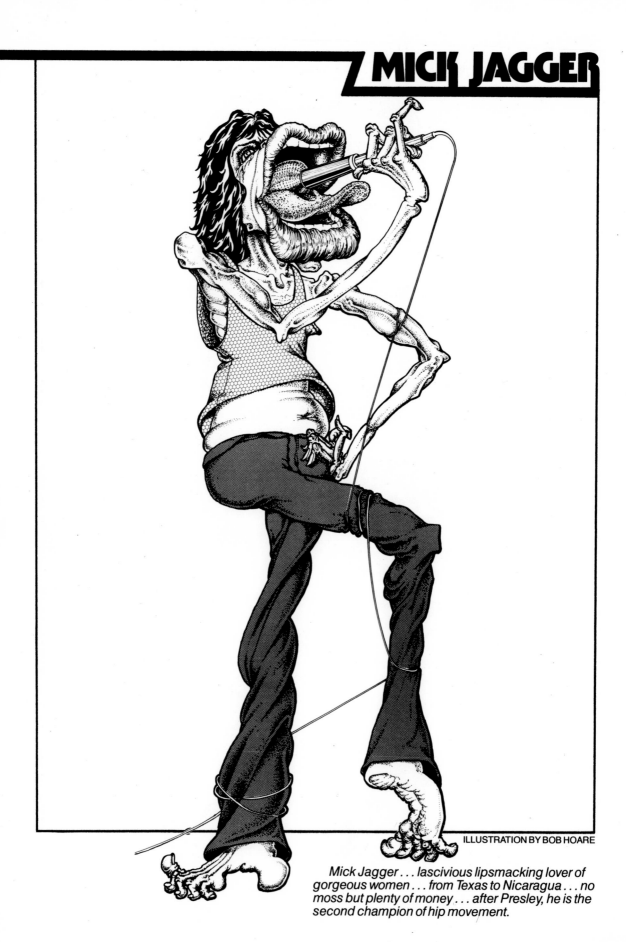

ILLUSTRATION BY BOB HOARE

Mick Jagger . . . lascivious lipsmacking lover of gorgeous women . . . from Texas to Nicaragua . . . no moss but plenty of money . . . after Presley, he is the second champion of hip movement.

DAVID BOWIE

ILLUSTRATION BY BOB HOARE

ILLUSTRATION BY BOB HOARE

ELVIS PRESLEY

ILLUSTRATION BY BOB HOARE

Elvis . . . the king . . . forerunner of the Empire State quiff brigade . . . from barnstorming boogie boy to Vegas viceroy . . . a coffin clad junk food victim, he lived and breathed rock 'n' roll.

ILLUSTRATION BY BOB HOARE

BUDDY HOLLY

ILLUSTRATION BY BOB HOARE